Pebble® Plus

EXTREME EARTH

T0044849

HOTTEST PLACES
ON THE PLANET

by Karen Soll

CAPSTONE PRESS
a capstone imprint

Pebble Plus is published by Capstone Press,
1710 Roe Crest Drive, North Mankato, Minnesota 56003
www.mycapstone.com

Library of Congress Cataloging-in-Publication Data
Soll, Karen, author.
  Hottest places on the planet / by Karen Soll.
    pages cm.—(Pebble plus. Extreme Earth)
  Summary: "Simple text and full-color photographs describe the hottest places on the
planet"-- Provided by publisher.
  Includes bibliographical references and index.
  ISBN 978-1-4914-8341-1 (library binding)
  ISBN 978-1-4914-8345-9 (pbk.)
  ISBN 978-1-4914-8349-7 (ebook PDF)
1. Climatic extremes—Juvenile literature. 2. Tropics—Juvenile literature. 3. Deserts—
Juvenile literature. 4. Earth (Planet)--Core--Juvenile literature. I. Title.
  QC981.8.C53S65 2016
  910'.913--dc23   2015025592

Editorial Credits
Karen Soll, editor; Juliette Peters, designer;
Tracy Cummins, media specialist; Tori Abraham, production specialist

Photo Credits
Alamy: Eric Chahi, 15, imageBROKER, 11, Kris Wiktor, 13; Getty Images: Tim Bewer, 9;
NOAA: Dr. Bob Embley/NOAA PMEL, Chief Scientist, 19; Shutterstock: Aleksandra H.
Kossowska, Cover Top Right, 3, Anton Prado, Design Element, 1, beboy, Cover Top Left,
Galyna Andrushko, Cover Bottom, Ivsanmas, Map, Johan Swanepoel, 21, samarttiw, 7,
22-23, ssguy, 5; Thinkstock: Dorling Kindersley, 17

Note to Parents and Teachers

The Extreme Earth set supports the Next Generation Science Standards related
to earth science. This book describes and illustrates climate and geography. The
images support early readers in understanding the text. The repetition of words
and phrases helps early readers learn new words. This book also introduces early
readers to subject-specific vocabulary words, which are defined in the Glossary
section. Early readers may need assistance to read some words and to use the
Table of Contents, Glossary, Read More, Internet Sites, Critical Thinking Using the
Common Core, and Index sections of the book.

Printed in the United States   5346

TABLE OF CONTENTS

HOT PLACES

Think about being outside
on a hot day. Some places
are hotter than others.
Let's find out which places
get really hot!

Bangkok, Thailand, gets very hot.

The air is wet and heavy.

It feels hotter than it is.

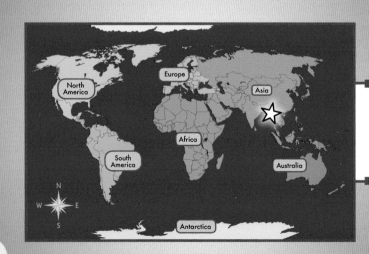

The average daytime temperature in Bangkok is 90 degrees Fahrenheit (32 degrees Celsius).

A valley in Ethiopia is like a bowl that traps heat. It is very hot. Just a few people have seen it.

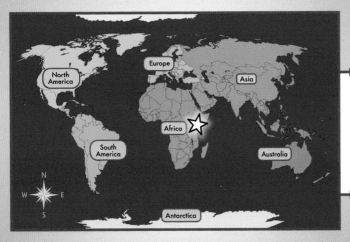

Dallol is a place that sits in the valley. The temperature in Dallol never drops below 93 degrees Fahrenheit (34 degrees Celsius).

HOTTER PLACES

What if your town

was hot for 160 days?

Marble Bar has that record.

This desert town is in Australia.

From October 31, 1923, temperatures reached above 100 degrees Fahrenheit (38 degrees Celsius) for 160 days.

Furnace Creek Ranch

is in California.

This hot place is in a desert

called Death Valley.

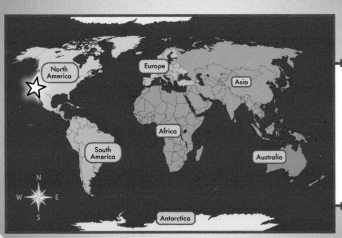

On October 7, 1913, the temperature at the ranch was 134 degrees Fahrenheit (57 degrees Celsius). This set a record for the hottest temperature in the western half of the world.

One place in the Sahara desert had a very hot day. It was the hottest day ever recorded. This happened in 1922.

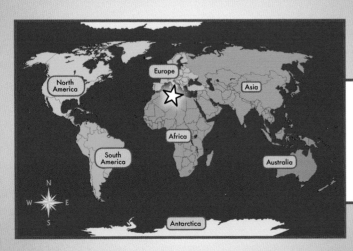

On September 13, 1922, the temperature in Al Aziziyah, Libya, was 136 degrees Fahrenheit (58 degrees Celsius).

HOTTEST PLACES

Molten rock in Earth

gets very hot. Rocks above

it crack. Water gets into

these cracks.

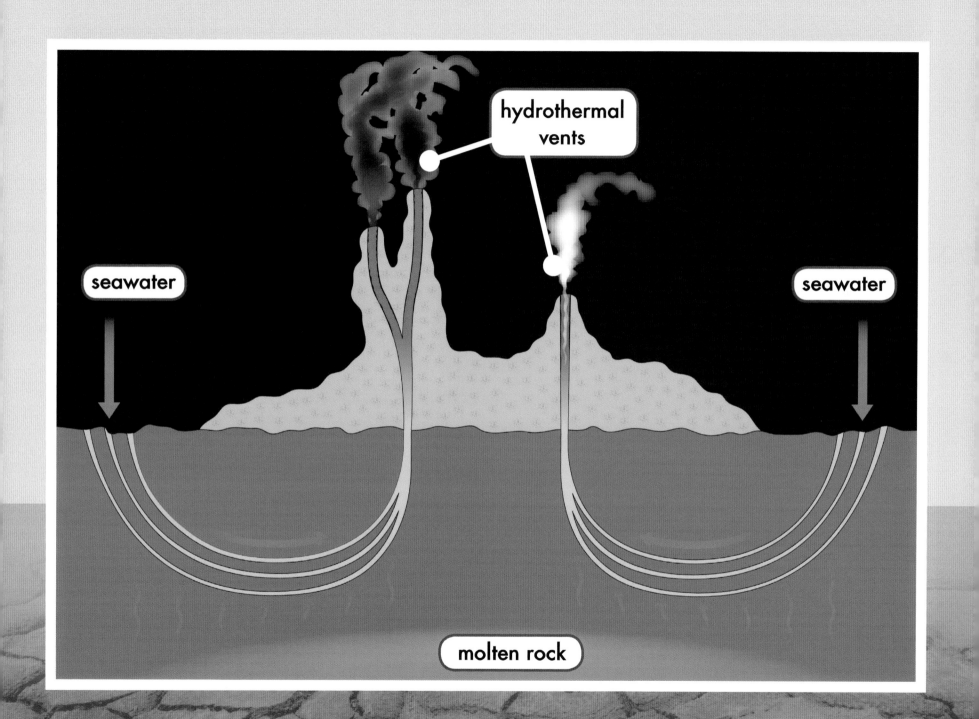

The water gets hot and bursts to the surface as steam. The steam is so hot it can melt lead.

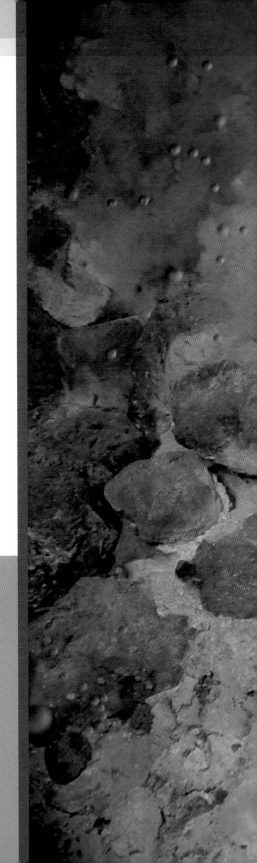

The hottest spot is Earth's core.

You can't see Earth's core.

There are other hot spots you

can visit. Which place would you

like to see?

Earth's core has a recorded temperature of 6,650 degrees Fahrenheit (3,677 degrees Celsius).

GLOSSARY

core—the inner part of Earth that is made of metal, rocks, and melted rock

desert—a dry area with little rain

melt—to change from a solid to a liquid because of heat

molten—melted by heat

recorded—written so it can be used or seen again in the future

steam—a hot gas from water that is heated

temperature—the measure of how hot or cold something is

valley—a low area of land between hills or mountains

READ MORE

Ganeri, Anita. *Harsh Habitats.* Extreme Nature. Chicago: Heinemann-Raintree, 2013.

Rustad, Martha E. H. *Earth's Hottest Place and Other Earth Science Records.* Wow! Mankato, Minn.: Capstone Press, 2014.

Simon, Seymour. *Seymour Simon's Extreme Earth Records.* San Francisco: Chronicle Books, 2012.

INTERNET SITES

FactHound offers a safe, fun way to find Internet sites related to this book. All of the sites on FactHound have been researched by our staff.

Here's all you do:

Visit *www.facthound.com*

Type in this code: 9781491483411

Check out projects, games and lots more at
www.capstonekids.com

CRITICAL THINKING USING THE COMMON CORE

1. How can a valley be like a bowl that traps heat? (Craft and Structure)

2. How is Marble Bar like another desert in this book? (Key Ideas and Details)

3. Draw a picture of how molten rock can cause steam. Label your picture. (Integration of Knowledge and Ideas)

INDEX

Grade: 1